Conducting Remote Audits

Steven M. Bragg

AccountingTools®

ISBN 978-1-64221-230-3

For more information about AccountingTools® products, visit our Web site at www.accountingtools.com.

Table of Contents

About the Author

Steven Bragg, CPA, has been the chief financial officer or controller of four companies, as well as a consulting manager at Ernst & Young. He received a master's degree in finance from Bentley College, an MBA from Babson College, and a Bachelor's degree in Economics from the University of Maine. He has been a two-time president of the Colorado Mountain Club, and is an avid alpine skier, mountain biker, and certified master diver. Mr. Bragg resides in Centennial, Colorado. He has written more than 300 books and courses, including *New Controller Guidebook*, *GAAP Guidebook*, and *Payroll Management*.

Steven maintains the accountingtools.com web site, which contains continuing professional education courses, the Accounting Best Practices podcast, and thousands of articles on accounting subjects.

Buy Additional AccountingTools Courses

AccountingTools offers more than 1,500 hours of CPE courses, with concentrations in accounting, auditing, finance, taxation, and ethics. Related courses that you might like include:

- Agile Auditing
- Guide to Analytical Procedures
- Guide to Data Analytics for Audits
- The Audit Risk Model

Go to accountingtools.com/cpe to view these additional courses.

AccountingTools®

Conducting Remote Audits

Introduction

A *remote audit* is comprised of audit activities that are performed at any location other than the location of the audited party. These audits may include both real-time work (such as video calls) and off-line work (such as document reviews). There are several variations on the concept, which are as follows:

- *Partially remote audit*. This is when the audit team finds that some portions of an audit must be conducted on-site, while some auditors are still able to work off-site, either fully or only on some days of the week. In these cases, the on-site staff may support the off-site staff, locating needed documents for them and lining up interviews on their behalf.
- *Expert remote audit*. This is when an expert who does not have time to be on-site conducts an analysis in his or her area of expertise from an off-site location, with other auditors providing on-site support. This is especially useful when experts are expensive or do not have sufficient time available to travel to and from clients.

Remote auditing has been around for a number of years, but advances in electronic communications technology now make it easier to implement.

There is an increasing need for remote audits. Audit firms are finding it more difficult to hire auditors who are willing to travel for extended periods of time, while travel costs are rising. In addition, the ongoing threat of pandemics presents the possibility that a regional shutdown may occur on short notice, rendering on-site audits impossible. Layered on top of these issues is demands by auditors for more work-life balance, where they can travel less and work more frequently from home.

In this manual, we cover the advantages and disadvantages of remote audits, and how they can be accomplished.

What is a Remote Audit?

The auditor conducts a remote audit using long-distance approaches to collecting audit evidence, including phone calls, email, and video conferencing. These techniques are intended to replace – to the greatest extent possible – on-site meetings and facility tours. This does not necessarily mean that an audit can be conducted entirely from a remote location; the auditor may still need to conduct some on-site work to ensure that all audit objectives have been completed. Nonetheless, following remote auditing principles can greatly reduce the amount of on-site time required for an audit engagement, if managed effectively.

Advantages of a Remote Audit

There are multiple advantages to using remote audits, as noted in the following bullet points:

- *Enhance efficiency*. Working remotely can greatly increase auditor efficiency, because travel time is eliminated. This can be a major factor, especially when clients are located long distances away from auditor homes. If auditor travel time can be reduced significantly, this may reduce auditor turnover, which in turn allows an audit firm to cut back on its recruiting expenditures.
- *Increase productive hours*. An add-on benefit of eliminating travel time is that the total number of productive hours worked by each auditor goes up. This means that an audit firm can get the same volume of work done with fewer auditors, which in turn reduces its recruiting costs, as well as its office space requirements.
- *Increase auditor pool*. As travel requirements decline due to remote auditing, an audit firm may find that its pool of potential auditor recruits increases. There may be fully qualified auditors available who are unable to travel for any number of reasons, such as family constraints. This means that an audit firm may find itself with two sets of auditors – those who work locally, and those willing to travel longer distances to client sites.
- *Increase supervisory time*. Remote audit tools are especially useful for sharing audit documentation and findings, and allowing audit supervisors to conduct work paper reviews remotely. This, in turn, can lead to substantial cuts in the travel time required by audit supervisors.
- *Avoid on-site audit room*. In cases where the audit team is entirely off-site, the client no longer needs to set aside a room for the audit team. This can be a notable advantage when the client is short on space.
- *Avoid on-site interruptions*. When working on-site, there is a temptation for the auditor to wander down the hall multiple times per day to drop in on a client and ask questions. This can be highly disruptive for the client, who has trouble getting into an efficient work rhythm. By shifting to off-site auditing, the auditor is forced to accumulate a list of questions and bring them up during a scheduled video call – which is more efficient for the client.
- *Reduced distractions*. Working from home can present fewer distractions for the auditor than working at the client, because there are fewer interruptions by fellow staff. However, this advantage can be frittered away when other members of the family are at home during the auditor's working hours. This can be a real concern when an auditor is interrupted during a discussion of controls or processes, leaving the person with an incomplete understanding of how a client operates.
- *Audit in difficult locations*. Yet another advantage is that remote auditing allows an audit firm to conduct audits within crisis areas, where there may be a high risk of terrorist attacks, war, or pandemics. However, this situation only arises when data links into the affected area are sufficiently robust to support routine video calls and data transfers.

- *Minimize audit notice.* A further advantage of remote auditing is that audits can be conducted with essentially no notice; that is, there is no advance warning related to someone making travel arrangements, or setting aside meeting rooms. Instead – and as long as the communication links are adequate – an auditor can call in to a remote location and immediately begin to conduct some types of audit procedures.

Disadvantages of a Remote Audit

The preceding list of advantages must be balanced against a number of problems associated with remote audits. These issues can include technology limitations, not being taken as seriously by client staff, miscommunications, and data privacy issues. Here are the main concerns:

- *Technology limitations.* There are situations in which it will simply not be possible to conduct audit tasks from a remote location. If the available remote-access technology is limited or not reliable, or the type of audit evidence needed mandates on-site work, then any opportunities for remote work will be quite limited. For example, if an auditor wants to work from a remote cabin, it is quite possible that video interviews conducted from that location will be interrupted due to connectivity issues, if they can be initiated at all.
- *Firewall blockages.* A client may have a firewall installed, which is a network device that monitors and filters incoming and outgoing network traffic based on the organization's security policies. The data transfers and video calls originating from within the company may trigger the firewall, causing it to block any traffic with the remote auditor. While this issue can be fixed by specifically granting the auditor system access, it can interrupt the flow of work until the blockage is remedied.
- *Home life limitations.* When auditors work from home, there may be ongoing interruptions by other family members, a pet, or even service people coming to the door. These interruptions need to be minimized to keep them from interfering not only with one's work, but also interactions with clients.
- *Confidentiality.* A client may be contractually prohibited from electronically sharing some of its documents, which eliminates any possibility of their remote examination. Also, the government may have imposed confidentiality laws that make it more difficult to share documents. At a minimum, the audit firm must ensure that all downloaded documents be protected.

Tip: Consider implementing a policy to delete all electronic files from the audit firm's system upon the conclusion of an audit – consistent with internal policies regarding work paper storage.

- *Missed clues.* A further concern is that the auditor will not see clues during video or phone calls with clients that would be readily apparent if these interviews had been conducted in person. Some aspects of body language, such as constant shifting, crossed arms, and an inability to look the auditor in the eye are lost during remote communications, which can deprive the auditor of key clues that something may be wrong.

- *Missing tone at the top*. An auditor who is never on-site is unable to observe client interactions, and will have only the most limited idea of the client's culture and *tone at the top* – the client's general ethical climate, as established by its board of directors and management team. Having a good tone at the top can help to prevent fraud and other unethical practices. Being on-site makes it much easier to spot a worried look on a client's face, or the negative vibe of a toxic workplace culture.

Tip: It may still be possible to obtain an understanding of the tone at the top from a remote location by making inquiries with the client's personnel, as well as by inspecting its training materials and new operating procedures, instructions, and so on.

- *Initial audits*. A remote audit is probably not a good idea for an initial audit. The initial audit is a good time to be on-site, meeting with key client personnel, touring the facility, and observing procedures. Once these baseline issues have been dealt with and recorded in the audit work papers, it is easier to selectively determine which aspects of the audit might be conducted remotely in the next year.
- *Sampling issues*. Sampling frequently requires an on-site presence, in order to judge whether sample documents are aberrations that need to be replaced with alternative selections. Sorting through samples online is not as easy, and could lead to a protracted sampling process that wastes time.
- *Integrity reduction*. It is possible that the client will provide video images of processes that show only the most pristine operating conditions, or set camera angles to frame the most desirable images of a work environment. The client may also make only certain staff available for interviews. Under these conditions, the auditor will gain a skewed view of the conditions at the client site.
- *Cost cutting emphasis*. There is a risk that the audit manager will attempt to use remote auditing primarily as a tool to cut the cost (and possibly the price) of an audit, thereby allowing the audit firm to submit lower bids for audit work. There is a risk that this mindset will result in the audit firm skipping key activities that require the on-site presence of an auditor, thereby reducing the quality of the audit work. In short, the cost-savings inherent in remote work could result in a poor-quality audit.
- *Not taken seriously*. Members of the client's staff will not take the audit as seriously as they would if an audit team were on the premises. This is because having auditors parked in your office asking questions imposes a fairly high level of pressure to get the work done.
- *Client multi-tasking*. It is possible that, during a phone or video call, a client will be multi-tasking, and therefore not giving you his or her full attention.

When this situation arises, the client may be distracted, which reduces the quality of responses and may also extend the duration of a call.

- *Intimidation*. Client personnel are uncomfortable with auditors under the best of circumstances, since they feel that they are being judged. This concern can be heightened when interviews are held online, where the auditor cannot use body language to calm down the interviewee. The result can be a certain reticence to impart information. Conversely, being on-site and simply taking a client out to lunch might have easily defused the same interview.
- *Miscommunications*. Yet another issue is that virtual communications present the possibility of miscommunications. When an audit and client are face-to-face, it is easier to delve into all aspects of an issue, so that both sides understand it thoroughly. This outcome is less likely when (at best) the communication is by video chat, since the avenue of communication is more restricted.
- *Data privacy issues*. There are special concerns involving the remote inspection of documents. There may be nationally-imposed legal restrictions on data privacy, making it more important for the auditor to ensure that all documents shared by the client will be reviewed and stored in a confidential manner.
- *Fraud*. A further concern with documents in a remote environment is that the client might be able to fraudulently alter documents, which may not be detectable to an auditor inspecting the image on his or her computer screen. This calls for extreme vigilance to detect changes and manipulations. This issue can be mitigated by ensuring that all documents coming from third parties be sent directly to the auditor, so that the client has no opportunity to adjust them.

Impact of Audit Standards

The audit standards do not provide any exceptions when audit work is conducted off-site. That is, you must meet the requirements of all standards, with no exceptions. If it is not possible to do so from an off-site location, then you should shift the areas of concern to on-site audits.

Remote Audit Tools

In order to be efficient, auditors working remotely must have high-bandwidth Internet access, as well as electronic work papers and a cloud-based audit management system that can be accessed by everyone on the audit team. It may also be necessary to establish a secure online document storage system (such as Dropbox, Google Drive, or Box). Also, video-conferencing tools such as Zoom or Skype, or at least high-quality phone access are needed to conduct interviews with client staff. In all cases, be aware of how to record conversations, since they may be used as audit evidence. Here are some additional considerations for setting up communications with clients:

- Does your web conferencing software mandate that you issue an invite to the client?
- Does the client have to download any web conferencing software in advance?

- Does the system offer a screen sharing option? This is useful for viewing documents and programs.
- Does the client need a webcam?
- Does the client have a functioning microphone?

These considerations need to be addressed before any client interactions begin, to keep the audit process from bogging down right away.

Tip: Check auditor lighting in advance. Some laptop cameras are of low quality, and will need to be supplemented with a better webcam, as well as external lighting.

When auditors will be working remotely but not from home, try to ensure that they are operating from a quiet workplace (such as an office, rather than a cubicle), so that no external noises intrude on video or phone calls. In addition, be sure to clear the area covered by the laptop's webcam, so that no confidential or inappropriate information can be perused by the client on the other end of a call.

A less frequently-used tool is the security camera or webcam. If these cameras are installed in strategic locations within a client's facility, the auditor can remotely observe a variety of accounting transactions by client staff, and can even record them as evidence that procedures are being followed properly. There can be client push-back over this issue due to privacy concerns, while the client may find that in-depth camera coverage within its facilities is cost-prohibitive. Nonetheless, it may be possible for the auditor to negotiate with the client regarding optimal locations for camera installations.

An essential tool for remote auditing is the *facilitator*. This person is a local employee or contractor who is not certified or trained as an auditor, but who works on-site and provides assistance to the remote auditor, fulfilling requests to assist with audit tasks. This person does not participate in audit findings or the development of work papers.

Tip: The audit firm should implement a procedure to review the off-site equipment and Internet connections of its staff, to ensure that each auditor is technologically capable of engaging in remote audit work. In addition, devise policies and procedures for how these personnel are to conduct their remote work.

In cases where the audit firm has been retained well in advance, it may be possible to gain ongoing read-only electronic access to the client's accounting system. This allows the audit team to conduct real-time auditing of the accounting system throughout the year. This approach is useful for conducting tests without the client having to be directly involved at all. It is also a good way to conduct unexpected audit procedures, which is an excellent way to spot instances of fraud.

It can be useful to examine the on-site work required for each audit, to determine specifically what issues are preventing the audit firm from conducting remote audit procedures. This review can result in measures to increase the proportion of remote work completed on future audits.

Remote Audit Planning

The use of remote audit tools and techniques should be stated in the audit plan, rather than being implemented in a haphazard manner. By doing so, you can make a determination during the planning phase of the audit regarding when auditors are expected to be working off-site, so that all parties can plan to have the appropriate tools available on those dates for the scheduled work.

When remote auditing work is stated in the audit plan, there should be a pre-assessment of whether the auditors can access client data and employees. If there are constraints on doing so, it is best to find out as early as possible, so that auditors can be scheduled for on-site work.

Tip: As part of the planning process, conduct an early test of connections to ensure that video calls can be made, and that client data can be accessed. This should include agreement on the protocols to be used to keep client data secure while it is being examined off-site, including the use of a password-protected portal through which all electronic files are transferred.

The audit plan should state whether local facilitators will be used; if so, the plan should state the specific tasks for which they are responsible.

Tip: Where possible, use facilitators from the prior year's audit, since they will already be familiar with the audit firm's requests, and so will be more efficient than a new facilitator.

The audit plan may require the inclusion of a contingency plan, in case the communication links between the auditor and client break down. This can be as simple as having a backlog of work available at all times for which the auditor has data immediately at hand. At a minimum, each auditor should be provided with the contact information for someone who is best able to restore the Internet connection.

The audit plan should itemize a list of documents and other information that the client commits to provide to the audit firm by the start of the engagement. Ideally, this information should be available several days before the scheduled start of the audit, so that the audit supervisor can follow up on lagging submissions before the audit work begins.

Internal Control Assessments

Part of an audit is an assessment of the client's system of internal controls. The auditor is required to obtain an understanding of those client controls relevant to an audit, and assess whether they have been designed effectively to prevent or at least detect and correct material misstatements that might be made in the financial statements. Further, the auditor must then determine whether these controls have been properly implemented. This information is needed in order to ascertain whether additional audit procedures might be effective in detecting any material misstatements that might exist.

This can be exceedingly difficult to achieve as part of a remote audit, though there can be creative ways to address the issue. For example, you could have a facilitator position a cell phone so that you can use a video feed to watch someone enter a password to access a client's accounting system. The video feed can be used to determine whether password access is correctly implemented, and would indeed lock an unauthorized user out of the system.

If it is not possible to use such innovative approaches, you will need to schedule an on-site review. If it is not possible for the audit staff to attend to this matter on site, it may be possible to bolster the audit plan with an increased number of substantive tests instead. In the worst-case scenario, where neither option is available, the auditors may be forced to declare a scope limitation when writing their audit report.

Fraud Risk Assessment

As part of the normal audit procedures, an audit team must make a risk assessment regarding the potential for fraud at a client. This assessment is made more difficult when using remote auditing, since it is more difficult to read the body language of client personnel when only their heads are visible on a video call. When this is the case, the audit manager will need to devise alternative measures to assess fraud risk, which may include conducting an on-site assessment.

Skepticism

A key factor when engaging in a remote audit (or any audit) is to exercise professional skepticism when planning and performing the audit, with the view that the client's financial statements may be materially misstated. A properly skeptical auditor will be alert to the presence of contradictory audit evidence, any issues that question the reliability of client documents, conditions indicating the presence of fraud, and any circumstances calling for additional audit procedures. Maintaining a skeptical viewpoint is needed to mitigate the risks of overlooking unusual circumstances, over-generalizing when drawing conclusions, and using inappropriate assumptions.

The Audit Risk Model

When devising an audit plan that incorporates remote work, it is useful to consider the *audit risk model*, which determines the total amount of risk associated with an audit, and describes how this risk can be managed.

The model incorporates three types of audit risk into the following equation:

Audit risk (AR) = Control risk (CR) × Detection risk (DR) × Inherent risk (IR)

Or,

$$AR = CR \times DR \times IR$$

The three types of audit risk included in the equation are expanded upon as follows:

- *Control risk*. This is the risk that potential material misstatements would not be detected or prevented by a client's control systems. When there are significant control failures, a client is more likely to experience undocumented asset losses, which means that its financial statements may reveal a profit when there is actually a loss. In this situation, the auditor cannot rely on the client's control system when devising an audit plan.
- *Detection risk*. This is the risk that the audit procedures used are not capable of detecting a material misstatement. This is especially likely when there are several misstatements that are individually immaterial, but which are material when aggregated. The outcome is that the auditor would conclude that there is no material misstatement of the financial statements when such an error actually exists. Increasing the quantity and especially the quality of audit procedures will reduce detection risk.
- *Inherent risk*. This is the risk that a client's financial statements are susceptible to material misstatements in the absence of any internal controls to guard against such misstatement. Inherent risk is greater when a high degree of judgment is involved in business transactions, since this introduces the risk that an inexperienced person is more likely to make an error. It is also more likely when significant estimates must be included in transactions, where an estimation error can be made. Inherent risk is also more likely when the transactions in which a client engages are highly complex, and so are more likely to be completed or recorded incorrectly. Finally, this risk is present when a client engages in non-routine transactions for which it has no procedures or controls, thereby making it easier for employees to complete them incorrectly.

Of these three risks, only detection risk is largely under the control of the auditor. There will always be some amount of detection risk, due to the inherent limitations of an audit. Since the audit procedures used as part of a remote audit may differ from those used in an on-site audit, the audit plan will need to consider whether the procedures being used will reduce the level of detection risk by a sufficient amount.

Evidence Obtained from the Work of Others

The audit supervisor may choose to use the work of a client's internal audit function to obtain audit evidence, or ask them to provide direct assistance to the engagement team. The extent to which these parties or their work can be used depends on their level of objectivity and competence, as well as whether they apply a systematic and disciplined approach to the conduct of their work. Incorporating a client's internal audit staff and its work into an audit can reduce the extent of the work performed by the auditor, and may serve to keep the audit team off the premises, but it does not reduce the auditor's responsibility for the audit opinion expressed.

The auditor may make use of the work of an individual or organization that has expertise in an area other than accounting or auditing. Examples of areas in which an auditor may choose to use the work of a specialist are:

- Actuarial calculations of benefit plan liabilities
- Estimates of environmental liabilities
- Estimates of oil and gas reserves
- Interpretations of complex tax compliance issues
- Interpretations of laws and regulations
- The valuation of financial instruments and nonfinancial assets measured at fair value

Making use of the work of an auditor's specialist can result in valid audit evidence, but the auditor is still solely responsible for the audit opinion expressed, not the specialist.

The extent to which the auditor elects to use the work of an auditor's specialist will depend on the following issues:

- The nature of the work to be conducted.
- The risks of material misstatements associated with the work to be conducted.
- The significance of the work to be performed in relation to the audit.
- The auditor's knowledge of the specialist's prior work.
- Whether the specialist will be subject to the auditor's quality control procedures.

The auditor also needs to consider the competence and capability of a specialist, since these issues can impact whether the work of the specialist will be adequate for the auditor's purposes. It is an open question as to whether specialists can take on somewhat more of the audit work when an audit team is trying to shift to remote auditing.

Remote Audit Training Issues

A specific skill set is required for remote audits, which accounting schools have not necessarily provided to their students. This means that new auditors should probably be prohibited from engaging in remote audits until they have spent some time on-site with clients, and then shadowed more experienced auditors while they conduct remote auditing sessions. Further, when a relatively inexperienced auditor is allowed to engage in remote auditing, it may make sense to have a more senior person sit in on a few sessions to provide advice on how to deal with clients. Another approach is to set up a simulated training session, where auditors can use the firm's preferred software and hardware setups, and walk through a variety of scenarios to enhance their comfort level with the remote auditing concept. These sessions should certainly address the most likely technology failures, such as a dropped Internet connection or the client's inability to use teleconferencing software.

Audit Team Supervision

The audit standards mandate that an audit supervisor adequately supervise the audit team. How can this be done when the team is scattered among a number of locations? The main solution is timely and regular communications. The audit supervisor should know which tasks will be addressed by his or her staff every day, and contact them in advance to discuss any issues that may arise. The supervisor can also conduct follow-up reviews at the end of each day, and be available to answer questions throughout the day – pretty much what a competent supervisor is expected to do during an on-site audit. The only difference is that all communications are remotely conducted.

If there is one area that the audit supervisor needs to focus on with an off-site audit team, it is the quality of evidence gathered. High-quality evidence reduces audit risk, so there should be ongoing discussions about what constitutes high-quality evidence, and how this can be discerned through a remote connection with a client site.

Note: An audit team is supposed to accumulate sufficient appropriate audit evidence to reduce the level of audit risk to an acceptably low level, in order to draw conclusions from which to derive an auditor's opinion. Audit evidence is mostly derived from audit procedures performed during an audit, but may also include information from previous audits, a client's quality control procedures, or the work of specialists. The *absence* of information, such as a refusal by the client to provide access to employees, can also be used as audit evidence.

Introduction to the Client

When remote auditing is used for the first time, it is essential to properly introduce the concept to each client. This means having an initial meeting in which you clearly state that this is a typical audit, where the same work will be conducted, though some tasks will be completed somewhat differently. This means that the auditors will still conduct interviews, review documents, and gather evidence. During this discussion, explain why remote auditing is being used, what technology will be employed, and how the audit team will interact with client personnel.

Scheduling Tips

Scheduling meeting time with client employees can differ somewhat from the relatively informal on-site audit process. In remote auditing, the auditor should rigidly adhere to a set schedule of calls. If you have scheduled several online meetings in a row, it will be necessary to conclude your business with each participant in a timely manner – otherwise, you will need to reschedule for another meeting to conclude the original agenda. Also, if the discussion leads to a conclusion that the client will need to conduct some research or pull another document and get back to you (a common occurrence), you will not be able to simply wait for an answer – you will need to reschedule the call. This may mean that you should leave some gaps in your interviewing schedule, into which you can slot rescheduled meetings.

Another concern with remote auditing is that it can be stressful. Staring at a computer screen all day, especially for video conferences, can be demanding. Consequently, build in frequent breaks where you can stand up, walk around, eat a snack, and so forth. Otherwise, your productivity and level of alertness will likely decline as the day progresses. In addition, it can be difficult to work overtime in a remote auditing environment, for the reasons just noted. Therefore, try to keep your working hours down to a reasonable level.

Communication Tips

The communications medium in a remote audit is not as good as an in-person encounter, so here are some tips for improving the level of communication:

- Log in early to ensure that your end of the connection is functioning.
- Initially ask whether the communication quality is acceptable; if not, fix it before proceeding.
- Suggest that the other party close his or her office door, in order to minimize noise levels and distractions.
- Speak clearly and slowly, so the other party is more easily able to understand your questions; be patient.
- If you are using a divided screen to show a document, shut down the extra screen once the document discussion is over; thus, maximize the screen on whatever is the main topic of conversation.
- If the client appears confused, try rephrasing the question.
- Provide a short summary of what you thought the other party said; this may require a few iterations until both parties fully agree on the summarization.

Dealing with a Remote Client

In today's distributed work environment, it is entirely possible that some members of the client's team (or all of them) have also shifted to remote work locations. One advantage of this is that the client's personnel are likely to have robust communications tools already in place. However, it may also mean that the client has altered its system of controls to accommodate its remote work force. For example, a client's controller may have eliminated some supervisory checks that were previously included in the closing process, such as reviews of all journal entries made. Or, the client's management team might have decided to forego a requirement to have two signatures on every check, given the difficulty of transporting checks to two off-site locations to have them signed. The auditor will need to be alert to these procedural and control changes, and adjust the audit plan accordingly when any changes are found.

Remote Inventory Observations

Remotely observing the end-of-period inventory count can be extremely difficult for an auditor working from a remote location. The auditor is normally expected to be on-site, poking through the inventory storage areas and overseeing how the client conducts the count. It may be possible to do this by connecting to a local facilitator who points a video camera as directed by the auditor, which calls for a live link in the warehouse and other counting areas; however, due to reception issues, this is not always possible. A further concern is being able to evaluate the physical condition of inventory from a live stream. The person operating the camera could be instructed to check for dust, or hold up inventory to the camera for closer inspection, so this is not an insurmountable issue.

A more challenging situation is when the client can only submit a recorded video of the physical inventory count. In this case, it would be relatively easy for the client to stage the video to avoid failures in the count, resulting in an inaccurate inventory valuation.

Tip: An ideal person to hold a camera during a live stream walk-through of inventory is someone not connected to the warehouse or accounting staffs, such as a member of the internal audit department or a facilitator not connected to the client. The intent is to find someone with a reasonable level of objectivity.

If a count is conducted and there are flaws in the auditor's analysis, then this could result in a scope limitation that prevents the issuance of an unqualified opinion – especially when the inventory investment is material. Consequently, it may be necessary to schedule an on-site inventory observation.

Electronic Confirmations

It is acceptable for the auditor to transmit a confirmation request by email, using a scanned electronic copy of a document that has been signed by the client. In this case, the client may have signed the physical document or used an electronic signature.

The sending of a confirmation request by email still presents the risk of interception, since the email address used may not be the correct one. The auditor can perform procedures to confirm that the email to which the confirmation is being sent is the correct one. In addition, it may be necessary to directly contact the presumed sender (such as by telephone) to validate the source and nature of the electronic confirmation.

If the confirmation is sent back by email, there is a risk relating to the reliability of the point of origin, since you cannot tell if someone other than the intended recipient has control of the originating email address. It may be possible to mitigate this risk by using a secure confirmation environment, as offered by some third-party providers. Confirmations obtained electronically are considered reliable audit evidence, as long as you are satisfied of the following:

- That the information obtained is a direct communication in response to a request;

- That the electronic confirmation process is secure and properly controlled; and
- That the information is obtained from a third party who is the intended respondent.

A further advantage of using a third-party electronic confirmation service is that confirmations can be initiated and returned in just a few days, as opposed to the weeks required for paper-based confirmations. Furthermore, because of the rapid turnaround time, the auditor no longer has to spend hours validating or authenticating the responding entity.

If the auditor plans to use a third-party electronic confirmation system, then it may be necessary to obtain an assurance trust services report on the system. There are three types of these reports, which are as follows:

- *SOC 1 report.* Reports on the design and operating effectiveness of controls relevant to user entities' internal control over financial reporting.
- *SOC 2 report.* Reports on the design and operating effectiveness of controls that affect the security, availability, and processing integrity of the system used to process users' data and the confidentiality and privacy of the information processed by the system.
- *SOC 3 report.* Reports on whether a system complies with specified trust services principles and criteria.

You can use this report to assess the design and operating effectiveness of the electronic and manual controls associated with that process. The system used should also receive ISO 27001 certification. This certification is a recognized standard for the establishment and certification of an information security management system. It specifies the requirements for establishing, implementing, operating, monitoring, maintaining and improving a system. This system should cover the online audit confirmation service and infrastructure, including data and data environments, servers, source code and internal networks.

Note: When using a third-party confirmation service, be aware of the difference between in-network and out-of-network responders. A confirmation service may have already established a network of responders (such as banks), which have already been authenticated. An out-of-network responder has not been validated, so the auditor is responsible for determining that the confirmation was sent to the correct party, who is authorized to issue a response.

Audit Documentation

Besides the normal documentation that an audit team prepares, it is useful to preserve copies of all electronic communications with clients, such as e-mails. This information is as useful as any verbal communications with a client, which are also noted in the workpaper documentation.

Remote Audit Evaluation

Once an audit has been completed, be sure to evaluate how much time was spent on each remote task, and compare it both to the budget and the historical expectation for the duration of the same task when it was conducted on-site. This analysis may reveal that some tasks are more efficiently completed on-site, which may result in an altered audit plan for the next year's audit. Other conclusions from this evaluation might include the following:

- It is more efficient to conduct an on-site audit
- The audit team requires more training in how to conduct a remote audit
- The audit team needs to use different video conferencing software
- The timing of calls with client personnel needs to be adjusted

Summary

It is important to note that a remote audit is not really an audit issue at all – it is a logistical one, where the intent is to minimize on-site work while still completing every aspect of the audit objectives. The outcome may very well be a hybrid audit, where some work is completed on-site, while other work is completed elsewhere. In many cases, it will not be possible to keep the level of audit risk down to an acceptable level while running an entirely remote audit.

Glossary

A

Audit risk model. A model that determines the total amount of risk associated with an audit, and describes how this risk can be managed.

C

Control risk. The risk that potential material misstatements would not be detected or prevented by a client's control systems.

D

Detection risk. The risk that the audit procedures used are not capable of detecting a material misstatement.

F

Facilitator. A local employee or contractor who is not certified or trained as an auditor, but who works on-site and provides assistance to the remote auditor.

I

Inherent risk. The risk that a client's financial statements are susceptible to material misstatements in the absence of any internal controls to guard against such misstatement.

R

Remote audit. Audit activities that are performed at any location other than the location of the audited party.

T

Tone at the top. A client's general ethical climate, as established by its board of directors and management team.

Index